Contents

Nature's Paradise

Marvellous Madagascar: Inside a Rainforest

Lungs of the Earth   8

Slash and Burn   10

Counting the Carbon: 2050   12

People of the Rainforest   14

Mining for Minerals: The Consequences   16

Black Gold   18

Trading Trees   20

Failing Harvests: 2100   22

Hotting Up: The Problem of Global Warming   24

Climate Change Catastrophe: 2200   26

Paradise Lost?   28

Glossary   30

Further Information   31

Index   32

Nature's Paradise

Imagine a place that teems with life. It is full of trees, waterfalls, rivers, animals, plants, noises, smells, sounds and movement. Hot and humid, wet and steamy, this place is home to an estimated 50 million different species, including bright scarlet macaws, beautiful jaguars and brilliant hummingbirds that can flap their wings 12,000 times a minute. This is the most bio-diverse environment on the planet. Welcome to the incredible rainforest.

Why are rainforests so important?

Deforestation threatens more than just the trees that are cut down. It affects every part of the life cycle, from tiny insects to humans.

Earth's green belt

For millions of years, the rainforests of the Earth have provided clean air for us to breathe. When we breathe out, we release a poisonous gas called carbon dioxide. Rainforest plants and trees absorb carbon dioxide and convert it into oxygen. Located in the warm central belt of the Earth, the rainforests survived the last ice age but now they are in danger and they are disappearing fast.

NUMBER CRUNCHING

The Amazon rainforest is the world's largest tropical rainforest. It covers 6 million square kilometres. Around half of all the world's known animals and plants live there.

Under threat

Scientists estimate that half of the world's rainforests have been destroyed in the last 25 years as a result of human activities. The rainforest is rich with valuable resources. Farmers clear the rainforest to use the land for cattle ranches and crops. Trees are cut down to provide timber for the construction industry. Large companies and governments make fortunes selling oil. All of this comes at an incredibly high price.

Fragile forest

Natural processes on Earth are often interlinked. When something happens, such as the rainforests disappearing, it can trigger a series of actions that can have devastating effects. This book looks at the chain of links between the causes and effects of rainforest destruction. Why are rainforests so special and what will happen if they disappear?

The jaguar is one of the species threatened with extinction if the rainforests disappear.

5

Marvellous Madagascar: Inside a Rainforest

Millions of years ago, the land of our planet was all joined together in one supercontinent that geologists have named Gondwanaland. When the continents split apart, the wildlife on each of the land masses developed very differently. The island of Madagascar saw the development of some very special species.

New species

The Madagascan rainforests are home to thousands of rare and unusual animals like the extremely slow-moving three-toed sloth and the mouse lemur, the world's smallest primate. It is estimated that 80 to 90 per cent of the 250,000 species in the island's rainforests do not exist anywhere else on Earth. In the last ten years alone, more than 600 new species have been found. However, this extraordinary biodiversity will be lost if the forests disappear.

6

What is a rainforest made up of?

Layers of the rainforest

There are four layers in a rainforest: the forest floor, the understory, the canopy and the emergent layer. Each layer is home to an amazing range of animals and plants. The forest floor gets very little light so this is mostly made up of decaying plants. The understory is between the forest floor and the canopy. Here you can find animals such as frogs, snakes, jaguars, tigers and capybaras. The canopy is made up of large trees and plants like ferns and orchids. The emergent layer is the realm of monkeys, bats and eagles.

The rainforest is home to plants and animals with medicinal uses. For example, tea tree oil is used as an antiseptic whilst the rosy periwinkle contains anti-cancer chemicals.

Scientists are currently studying the toxins in the poison dart frog to see if they can be used to treat heart attacks.

What happens next?

⚠ Rainforests are the most species-rich places on the planet. A single rainforest in South America has 18,000 different types of plant.

⚠ Nearly all of our medicines are made from plants. Cures for serious illness such as cancer and AIDS may be found in the rainforests one day, but not if the habitats for these plants are destroyed.

Lungs of the Earth

Tropical rainforests are found in the regions above and below the Equator. Brazil, Indonesia, Borneo and the Democratic Republic of Congo have the largest rainforests in the world. There are no seasons in the Tropics, it is hot and wet all the time. Much of the wildlife that lives in the rainforests cannot survive anywhere else. It is adapted to the conditions there. Rainforests are so important, they even regulate the Earth's climate.

Why are rainforests called the lungs of the Earth?

In the balance

All mammals breathe in oxygen and breathe out carbon dioxide. All plants do the opposite: they breathe in carbon dioxide and through a process called photosynthesis, they turn it into oxygen. As mammals, humans and the natural world live in balance with each other. If something happens to change this balance, all life on Earth is affected.

Rapid change

Around 60 to 100 million years ago, most of the world's land mass was covered in rainforests. Now, only 6 per cent is. Nearly half of all remaining rainforests are in South America. This is partly due to the Earth's climate changing and becoming drier. It is also due to human activities such as mining and deforestation.

In Peru, illegal gold mining along the Madre de Dios river is causing environmental damage. It is also causing a conflict between neighbouring tribes.

The La Fortuna waterfall cascades from the rainforest in Costa Rica. Environmental campaigners argue that the rainforest is a natural paradise that needs protecting before it is too late.

Every minute, a piece of rainforest the size of 20 football fields is destroyed or damaged somewhere in the world. Per year, more than 100,000 square kilometres of rainforest are lost forever. That is an area five times the size of Wales.

Climate control

With destructive human activities increasing and more industrial development, we are creating more carbon dioxide. Plants and trees absorb some of this but the ground beneath a dense rainforest can absorb and store huge amounts. This is called a carbon sink. It means that rainforests are the planet's greatest natural climate controllers. Scientists estimate that rainforests absorb nearly 20 per cent of excess carbon dioxide. However, when the forests are cleared and burned, all the stored carbon dioxide is released back into the atmosphere with huge consequences for human health and the environment.

Every day, thousands of hardwood trees from rainforests are cut down. This truck carries logs out of the rainforest in Ecuador.

Slash and Burn

The greatest threat to the rainforest is from deforestation. The quickest way to clear land of ancient rainforest is called 'slash and burn'. Enormous bulldozers 'slash' down the mighty trees and fires 'burn' the remains. Birds and animals are forced to flee and have to adapt to new habitats. But what is all the new land used for?

The River Amazon snakes and twists through the lush rainforest.

Why is rainforest land cleared?

Fast food farming

In South America, much of the reclaimed rainforest land is used for grazing cattle. Today, it is estimated that more than 100 million cattle graze on land that was once Amazon rainforest in an area larger than France. These cattle are bred for the West's enormous fast food industry. The beef is reared in Brazil and then sent to the United States and other countries to be made into hamburgers and pet food.

NUMBER CRUNCHING

Every year, Americans eat 40 billion hamburgers. That is 3 per person per week.

Thousands of hectares of rainforest are slashed and burned each year to clear the ground for grazing cattle or planting crops.

Choking with smoke

In Indonesia rainforests are cleared so that the land can be used for palm oil plantations. Palm oil is used in many products from soap to fast food. In most years since the mid-1990s, these deliberate fires have caused enormous clouds of choking smoke and led to severe health problems for millions in the region. The air-polluting hazes have led to an increase in illnesses linked to breathing.

Side effects of burning

With thousands of years of nutrients and plant growth, the soil in a rainforest is extremely rich and fertile. However, after burning the soil is very poor. Thin grass for grazing can grow, but the thousands of cattle quickly graze the ground dry again. Crops cannot be grown on the same piece of land for long so more forest has to be cleared, causing even more destruction.

Palm oil is worth more to the Philippines than the rainforest. The forests are destroyed to grow oil palm trees.

Counting the Carbon: 2050

It is 2050. The Amazon rainforest is still being cut down. The land is worth more to businesses and farmers than keeping the trees, animals and ecosystems intact. Governments and charities have been working for decades to stop the rainforest being cut down but time is running out. The practice of slash and burn is continuing, causing carbon dioxide levels to rise at an alarming rate.

The Sumatran tiger is almost extinct. Its natural rainforest habitat is disappearing fast.

NEWS HEADLINES

Most food plants are grown in special greenhouses where the oxygen and carbon dioxide levels are carefully controlled.

Hundreds of species are becoming extinct. The last known Sumatran tiger has died and the remaining manatees are in captivity. There are no known jaguars left.

The weather forecast gives a daily 'carbon count' so people know the pollution levels.

Many people carry oxygen bottles with them, especially on smoggy days.

Millions of people worldwide have developed asthma as a result of the smoke clouds. The young and old are particularly vulnerable.

Coastal areas where protective rainforest once stood are now vulnerable to storms and flooding.

There is no stop to the logging industry and, as developing nations flourish, demand for hardwoods is as high as ever.

Despite environmentalists' warnings of dire consequences, rainforests are still being destroyed.

People of the Rainforest

Deep in the most remote parts of the world's rainforests live groups of people who know these environments inside out. They are traditional tribes of hunter-gatherers who live in balance with the forests. With their own language, culture and ways of living, the future of the indigenous people of the rainforest is as uncertain as that of the forest itself.

What will happen to the rainforest tribes?

Life in the forest

The Yanomami are an ancient tribe who live in the Amazon in Venezuela and Brazil. They live simply in large wooden huts and hunt for food in the rivers and rainforest. They are poor by Western standards but they do not need money to buy and sell goods. However, their way of life is under threat and their very survival hangs in the balance.

The Yanomami have huge knowledge about the rainforest in which they live. They use about 500 plants for food, medicine and house building.

Fight for survival

The rainforest is full of natural riches such as oil, gold, emeralds and valuable hardwood trees. As the oil-drilling, mining and logging companies move in, the Yanomami are forced to leave their homes. Their entire way of life is destroyed and they have no means of getting food. These tribal people cannot simply move to towns or cities to live. They speak different languages for one thing, but more importantly, they are not immune to our diseases.

If the Yanomami lose their lands, we all lose: the world will lose their vital knowledge of the plants and animals of the forest and their unique culture.

This child's face has been painted in tribal patterns with dye made from curucum seeds. Such traditions will be lost forever if the rainforests disappear.

The tribes who live in the Amazonian rainforest use materials from the surrounding rainforest to build their homes.

What happens next?

⚠ The Democratic Republic of Congo rainforest lies in central Africa. It is the world's second largest rainforest, an area around twice the size of France. More than 50 million people depend on it for survival. The United Nations and other international organisations and campaign groups are working to protect native rainforest peoples but it will take many governments to agree to make their future secure.

Mining for Minerals: The Consequences

The value of the rainforest can be measured in terms of its mineral wealth. With large oil reserves as well as gold and gemstones, logging and mining companies are taking over vast areas of rainforests all over the world. But what impact are they having and what are the consequences for us and the environment?

What effect does mining have on the rainforest?

City of gold?

In the past, some explorers believed that there was a beautiful city built entirely of gold called El Dorado ('the golden one') hidden away in the rainforest of the Amazon. The city itself was a myth but there was gold. Today, the gold and emerald mines of South America are grim places. There is almost no health and safety for workers or environmental protection. To extract gold, poisonous mercury is used and this is harmful for the workers and for the rivers that wash it away.

Gold mining in the Peruvian Amazon has a huge environmental impact and leaves a scar on the land (as seen here in this satellite photo).

An increase in logging and industry in the forest means more roads, more traffic, more pollution and more environmental impact.

The River Amazon holds 20 per cent of the world's freshwater and 1,000 other rivers flow into it from all over South America. The Amazon is becoming more and more polluted with mercury and this is having a massive impact on marine and forest animal life. Birds are eating infected fish, animals are drinking contaminated water and the whole food chain is being affected.

Building in the forest

As more industries invade the forest, there is a knock-on effect for other kinds of development. More access roads need to be built which means more deforestation. Towns spring up with homes and facilities for the workers. Trees are cleared to build airstrips to move precious goods out as fast as possible. All this development causes deforestation, water pollution and a loss of habitat for thousands of species.

Forest roads are little more than mud tracks. The more traffic that uses them, the more the land erodes.

Black Gold

One of the biggest and most destructive human activities affecting global rainforests is the drilling for oil, or 'black gold' as it is known. Such is the industrial world's need for oil that any new mineral reserves are extremely valuable. Nearly a quarter of all the oil imported to the United States comes from oil exploration in the Amazon. Oil drilling has brought wealth and jobs to the rainforest, but it has also brought environmental problems and consequences for human health.

What effect does drilling for oil have on the land?

The oil industry has a huge impact on the environment, from extraction and shipping to processing and refining.

Oil spills

All over the Amazon, there are towns and settlements that have been devastated by oil extraction. In Ecuador, virgin forest near the town of Tena has been ruined by oil drilling. The forest was killed off by poisonous oil that seeped everywhere.

In October 2000, more than five thousand barrels of oil spilled into the River Marañon in Peru, polluting a vast area. Some of the oil spread into a protected area of rainforest and caused huge damage. For the 20,000 people who depend on the river and its water, it was devastating. Fish catches became tiny. Lots of people developed skin diseases and stomach complaints from drinking and washing in the polluted water.

The endangered pink dolphin, the bôto, lives in the murky waters of the Amazon. Its future is under threat with the destruction of the rainforest.

Web of life

When the rainforests and rivers are polluted, the whole ecosystem and food chain is disrupted as desperate animals try to find new food sources and new habitats.

What happens next?

⚠ In 2010, the government of Ecuador signed a deal to not drill for oil in its rainforests. In return for not drilling, the country received more than US$3 billion from the United Nations. It is the first agreement of its kind and, environmental campaigners argue, could work in other rainforest regions of the world, too.

There are many large-scale oil operations extracting oil from the Amazon, such as this one in Manaus, Brazil.

Trading Trees

Plantations are large fields used to grow a single crop, such as bananas or rubber. The biggest crop from the rainforest is the trees themselves. The logging of these trees also doubles up as land clearance. Scientists estimate that 19 million precious rainforest trees are cut down every day to make way for crops or as part of the logging industry.

How is the rainforest cleared so quickly?

Industrial scale

Modern machines can fell trees and remove vegetation that has taken hundreds of years to grow and develop into a complex environment. Enormous bulldozers and logging lorries make swift work of the rainforest. Once the main trees have been cleared and sent for sale, other machines move in to build new roads. This makes it easier and quicker to get into the forest to fell even more trees. Many people in countries with rainforests are poor, so selling their valuable wood is how they make a living.

The island of Borneo has one of the highest deforestation rates in the world. More than a million hectares of rainforest are cut down every year.

There are now more than 8 million hectares of soya beans growing in the Amazonian region.

Winners and losers

After the trees have been removed from an area of rainforest, crops such as soya beans are often planted. This is a valuable crop and is used for cattle feed all over the world. Whilst one industry may gain from the forest clearances, another suffers potentially huge losses. Around 25 per cent of Western medicines are derived from rainforest ingredients. Scientists estimate that we have explored and tested about 1 per cent of the trees and plants of the rainforests. With every tree that is cut down, we perhaps lose a chance to find a cure for a devastating disease.

What happens next?

⚠ The most valuable trees in a rainforest are ebony and teak. Their wood has a range of uses, from making furniture and boats to sculptures and musical instruments. The tropical hardwood trade is worth millions of pounds to the traders. Organisations like Friends of the Earth ask people to not buy furniture made from tropical hardwoods as this helps to stop deforestation.

Failing Harvests: 2100

It is 2100. A new century begins. Usually, it is a time of celebration but there's not much to celebrate. With further rainforest clearances and rising global temperatures, the weather has become much more unpredictable and extreme. Fierce storms batter huge areas of the world's land, washing away soil nutrients. Harsh droughts affect other areas, killing off bacteria which nourish the soil. The planet's farmland is less fertile than it was a century ago: how is enough food going to be grown to feed everybody?

Extreme weather batters the planet. Land and cities are flooded, crops are ruined and people have to leave their homes.

Human food supplies are running out. Drought-stricken land can't provide enough crops to feed the global population.

Rainforest clearance has left the land loose and unstable, so landslides like this one in Costa Rica are a common sight. Many people have been killed.

The soil is too thin to support the crops. It's becoming infertile and doesn't bind together.

In many parts of the world, strong winds make dustbowls and the crops are blown away.

Farmers abandon useless land in search of more fertile fields which means clearing more rainforest.

Farmers use more and more fertilisers and pesticides on the soil but it washes off into the rivers, killing fish and affecting freshwater supplies.

Scientific warnings that fewer rainforests would mean less rain have become a reality. Crops have to be watered by machine, putting pressure on the Earth's freshwater supplies.

Fresh food prices have rocketed but the quality has slumped. Poor soil quality means that the food isn't vitamin-rich anymore.

Lots of people have to take artificial food supplements to make up for low vitamins in real food. They eat food pills to keep healthy.

Hotting Up: The Problem of Global Warming

Everything about our natural world depends on a healthy balance between humans and their environment. But when our actions create an imbalance then everything starts to change. Large-scale deforestation coupled with industrial pollution have serious consequences for the future of our planet's climate.

What does global warming mean for the rainforests?

The greenhouse effect

Everybody loves a sunny day but a permanently over-heated planet would not be as welcome. Usually, the Sun warms the Earth and then heat from the Earth travels back up into the atmosphere. If everything is in balance, the heat passes through the atmosphere into space and the Earth is kept at a constant temperature.

The South Pole, shown here from space, is shrinking fast. As it is melting, the planet is losing its natural climate control and becoming hotter and hotter.

24

If there are too many 'greenhouse gases' like carbon dioxide in the atmosphere, the heat cannot escape and it is trapped, just as the windows of glass in a greenhouse trap in heat. This means the planet starts to heat up. The consequences of this are enormous: extreme weather, drought, melting ice caps, flooding and failed harvests.

There are eight species of hornbill found in the rainforests of Borneo. The removal of trees where they nest is having a huge impact on their population.

Natural balance

By absorbing carbon dioxide, rainforest vegetation helps keep the planet cool. But rainforests are themselves under threat from global warming. Scientists warn that if the planet gets hotter and drier, rainforests will dry up and the plants will wither even before they are cut down.

What happens next?

⚠ Scientists in Borneo have grown a rainforest from scratch using seeds from more than 1300 trees. Now, fewer than 5 years later, more than 30 types of mammal and 116 types of bird have moved in. This raises hopes for the future of the rainforests. The United Nations is looking at creating more new rainforests as a way of balancing the climate. Only time will tell if it is successful.

Climate Change Catastrophe: 2200

It is 2200. The last tree in the last rainforest on Earth has been cut down. The planet stands on the edge of climate disaster...

Rising sea levels have meant that most of the islands of the Maldives have disappeared into the ocean. Experts take tourists on diving trips to explore the islands that are underwater.

Some parts of India are permanently flooded. People have had to flee to higher ground and make their homes there.

Many parts of the world lie beneath a thick blanket of snow and ice. It is a struggle for people and animals to survive.

weather is happening all over the world. Mass chaos and misery is caused by freak rain, drought, snow and ice.

....

Wind patterns have changed along with temperatures, so grapes are now grown in sunny northern Russia and Britain is covered in permanent frost and ice.

....

People live in small communities in purpose-built atmosphere controlled blocks.

....

Outside, people wear oxygen masks.

....

People work mainly from home and rarely travel.

....

The map of Britain looks very different now. London has disappeared under water as has most of Cornwall and East Anglia.

....

People have moved inland to higher ground.

....

Governments fight over what to do and go to war over what resources there are left.

....

27

Paradise Lost?

According to scientists, if the rainforests continue to be destroyed at the current rate, and if the planet keeps getting hotter, by 2150 there will be almost no rainforests left. Because of the knock-on effects of global warming, melting ice caps, rising sea levels and a change in the level of carbon dioxide in the air, this would be disastrous for all life on Earth. We are running out of time to save these vital oxygen-giving forests.

What can be done to protect the rainforests?

Learning lessons

In the last 200 years, most of Australia's rainforests have been replaced by farms and towns. However, scientists are now studying the remaining forests and learning how these complex ecosystems work. For example, if the southern cassowary bird becomes extinct (it is already endangered), so will around 150 rainforest trees and plants that rely on it to spread their seeds. There is no other creature that can do this. So we do not just lose one creature, we lose a whole ecosystem.

A conservation plan has now been put in place to help save the southern cassowary bird. Scientists are working on ways to protect the bird and preserve its habitat.

Earth Day

On 22 April 1970, the first Earth Day took place. This annual event raises awareness of environmental issues including rainforest protection. Each year, there is a different campaign.

These girls live in Boca de Valeria on the River Amazon in Brazil. The rainforest is home to many people, animals and plants but is also the lungs of the Earth, providing us with oxygen.

What happens next?

⚠ Your decisions and actions really can make a difference and can change the world. If you would like to get involved you could join a rainforest protection campaign or organise an Earth Day event at your school. You could find out about an endangered rainforest animal or tribe. You could choose to sponsor a tree or not buy products made from tropical hardwood. Campaigners say we all need to act and do our bit to be great guardians of the planet for future generations. After all, there is only one Earth, so let's look after it.

Glossary

bio-diverse range of animals and plants in a particular place

captivity living in a confined conservation area

carbon sink rainforest or plantation that absorbs carbon dioxide in large quantities

climate type of weather a place normally gets at different times of the year

contaminated polluted

continents land masses: Europe, Africa, North America, Asia, South America, Antarctica, Australia

deforestation deliberate cutting down of forests to use land for grazing or agriculture

derived from comes from

dustbowls areas where vegetation has been lost and soil eroded, usually as a result of drought or poor farming methods

ecosystem plants, animals and the environment they inhabit together

Equator invisible circle around the middle of the Earth where the temperature is constant

excess leftover

food chain feeding relationships between living things

geologists scientists who study the structure of the Earth including its rocks and soils

global warming average increase in temperature at the Earth's surface

greenhouse effect when heat from the Sun enters the Earth's atmosphere and is trapped, heating up the planet

greenhouse gases gases such as carbon dioxide and methane in the atmosphere, which traps the Sun's heat and so causes global warming

habitat home environment, where something lives

hardwood wood from broad-leaved trees such as oak, beech and elm

hunter-gatherers people who live by hunting animals and gathering edible plants

immune safe from disease

indigenous belonging to or coming from a certain place

mammal warm-blooded animal

nutrients vitamins and nourishment

photosynthesis process by which plants change carbon dioxide and water into food using energy from the Sun

pollution contamination or poisoning of natural resources such as water or soil

primate large-brained mammals such as humans, apes and monkeys

tropics countries that are located above and below the Equator

vegetation plants

virgin forest untouched forest where no development has taken place

Further Information

Books

100 Facts on Rainforests, Camilla de la Bedoyere, Miles Kelly Publishing, 2009

Bloomin' Rainforests, Anita Ganeri and Mike Phillips, Scholastic, 2008

Eco Alert: Rainforests, Rebecca Hunter, Franklin Watts, 2012

Kingfisher Readers: Rainforests, James Harrison, MacMillan, 2012

Planet Earth: Rainforests, Steve Parker, ED Publishing, 2009

What Happens If the Ozone Disappears? Mary Colson, Wayland, 2013

Websites

www.earthday.org
If you would like to play your part and get involved in Earth Day on April 22 each year visit this website to find out more.

www.rainforest-alliance.org
Visit the treehouse at this interactive website and learn all about the rainforest. There's lots of other fun stuff such as rainforest games and quizzes.

www.foe.co.uk
Have a look at Friends of the Earth's anti-hardwood campaign at this website.

Index

Amazon rainforest 4, 10, 12

Amazon River 17, 29

animals 4, 5, 6, 7, 10, 12, 13, 15, 17, 19, 25, 27, 28, 29

biodiversity 6, 25

Borneo 8, 25

Brazil 8, 10, 14

carbon dioxide 4, 8, 9, 12, 13, 25, 26

carbon sink 9

cattle ranches 5

climate 8, 24, 25

climate change 26-27

Costa Rica 23

deforestation 4, 8, 10, 17, 21, 24

Democratic Republic of Congo 8, 15

El Doradao 16

Equator 8

extreme weather 25, 27

food chain 17, 19

freshwater 17, 23

gold 15, 16

greenhouse effect 24

greenhouse gases 25

hamburger industry 10

hardwood 15, 21, 29

logging 15, 16, 20-21

Madagascar 6-7

Maldives 26

medicine 7, 21

minerals 16-17, 18

mining 8, 15, 16-17

oil 5, 15, 16, 18-19

palm oil 11

photosynthesis 8

pollution 11, 13, 17, 18, 19, 24

rainforest people 14-15, 18

slash and burn 10-11, 12

soil quality 11, 22, 23

tropics 8

Venezuela 14